C000259662

we ♥love you...

Justin

AN UNAUTHORISED 2012 ANNUAL

Written by Martin Johnston
Designed by Nicky Regan

£7.99

CONTENTS

...you're so talented!
...we love all your songs!

...your beautiful hair!
...you have so much talent!

WE LOVE YOU BECAUSE...
WHY? WELL, BECAUSE...
...you're the best ever!

...you're extra special!

...we are Beliebers!

we love you...
Justin

WHAT'S ON JUSTIN'S iPOD... TOP TUNES!

What tunes do you think are on Justin's iPod? These are some of the artists that influenced his sound:

Ne-Yo:	*there from the start!*
Usher:	*of course!*
Stevie Wonder:	*the greatest?*
Boyz II Men:	*those harmonies!*
Michael Jackson:	*like Justin, the complete package.*

CANADA

First big appearance: Urban Behavior tour, West Edmonton Mall, Edmonton, Canada, November 3, 2009. (Should have been at Metrotown in Vancouver on November 1 but Justin had to pull out due to illness)

NEW YORK

First really dazzling appearance: Macy's 4th of July Fireworks Spectacular, New York City, USA, July 4 2010.

AROUND THE WORLD
WITH JUSTIN

Justin is a massive hit around the world, so he has to keep up a hectic, globetrotting lifestyle to reach all his Beliebers...

BIRMINGHAM

First massive English gig: National Indoor Arena, Birmingham, UK, March 4, 2011.

CONNETICUT

First big solo tour date: My World Tour, XL Center, Hartford, Connecticut, USA, June 23, 2010. My World tour goes on to visit: 18 more countries including Israel, Australia, Japan and Singapore!.

I'M A BELIEBER...

"*You're lovely, you're a great singer – and an amazing dancer!*" Danni Gurl

"*Peace, luv, bacon and Justin Bieber.*" Bieber Fan

"*I love himmmmmm!!! I love Justin Bieber!!!!!*" bb417

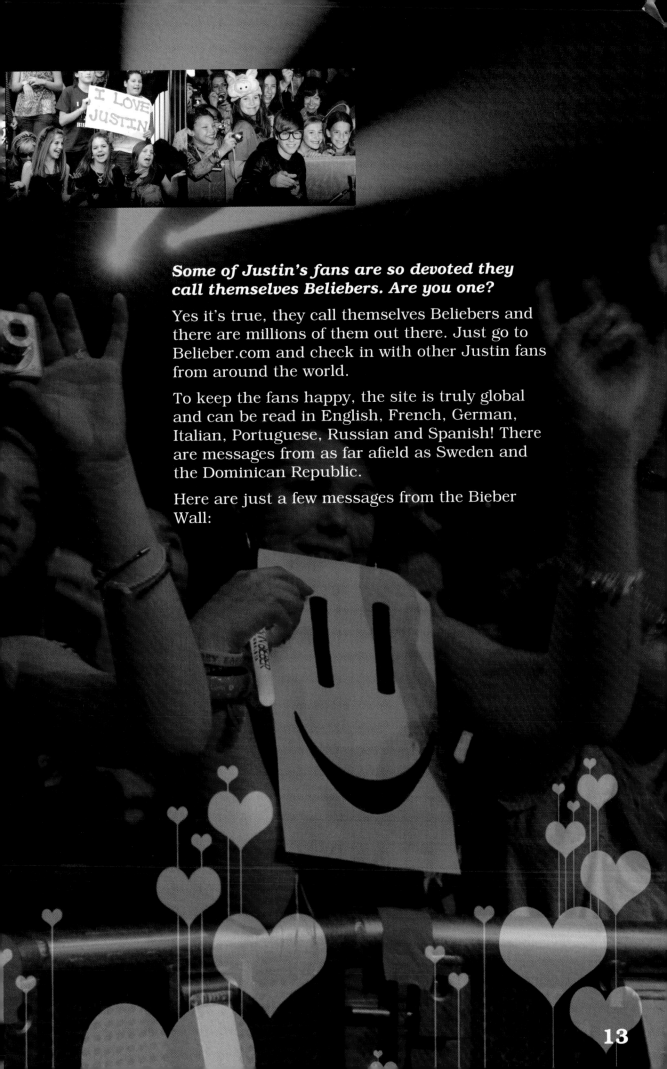

Some of Justin's fans are so devoted they call themselves Beliebers. Are you one?

Yes it's true, they call themselves Beliebers and there are millions of them out there. Just go to Belieber.com and check in with other Justin fans from around the world.

To keep the fans happy, the site is truly global and can be read in English, French, German, Italian, Portuguese, Russian and Spanish! There are messages from as far afield as Sweden and the Dominican Republic.

Here are just a few messages from the Bieber Wall:

SPOT THE DIFFERENCE

Study these two pictures of Justin closely. Can you spot the eight differences between the two?

Mark them on the bottom one.

Tip: use a pencil so you don't ruin your annual!

Answers on page 60.

we ♥ love you... Justin

16

1 In which Canadian town was Justin born?

2 In which U.S. city did the My World tour begin?

3 What is Justin's middle name?

4 In which city did Justin play his first UK gig on the My World tour?

5 The daughter of which Hollywood star supported Justin on his UK dates for the My World tour?

6 What star sign is Justin?

7 By what name is Justin's mum commonly known?

8 What was Justin's first single?

9 Which well-known US rapper features on Baby?

10 Justin sang a version of K'naan's Wavin' Flag to support earthquake victims in which country?

11 In 2010 Justin sang live on what hit UK TV show?

12 What is Justin's first film called?

13 What Brit Award did Justin win in 2010?

14 How many Grammy awards was Justin nominated for in 2010?

15 What was the name of Justin's second official DVD release?

16 What is the last song on the album My World 2.0?

17 In which Canadian city should Justin have started the Urban Behavior tour in 2009?

18 To which record label is Justin signed?

19 What is Justin's exclusive fragrance called?

20 In which UK city was Justin ordered to stay inside his hotel in case his fans caused a riot?

THE BIG BIEBER QUIZ

Justin has worked with some of the biggest and best names in the music industry including:

Willow Smith
Daughter of Hollywood star Will Smith, only 10 years old and already a superstar in her own right – supported Justin on his UK tour in 2011 and featured in the smash hit Whip My Hair.

Ludacris
Rapper (aka Christopher Brian Bridges) with four number one albums and two number one singles to his name in his native USA. Worked with Justin on his massive hit Baby.

Usher
The man behind Justin. The man who discovered him and made him the superstar he is today – also a music megastar in his own right. Has had eight US number one singles and each of his last four albums has gone to number one.

Justin has also featured on songs by Chris Brown, Soulja Boy and Sean Kingston.

Ludacris

Usher

Sean Kingston

BIEBER'S
BEZZIES!

Willow

Chris Brown

Soulja Boy

19

When he's not on the road playing massive shows in exotic locations, Justin is the same as all of us.

He just loves to chill at home. Watching or playing his favourite sport of ice hockey, known as just 'hockey' in Canada, where it is the national sport.

Home is with his mother Pattie in Stratford, Ontario, Canada, though Justin was born in London! (London, Ontario that is! One of Canada's biggest cities that was named after our capital).

AT HOME WITH
THE BIEBERS

JB is for... *just beautiful!*

JB is for... *jazzy beats!*

JB IS FOR...

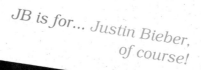

JB is for... *Justin Bieber, of course!*

Can you find the 19 hidden Justin Bieber-related words here in our tricky little word search? Don't forget words can be forwards, diagonal or even backwards. Good luck!

BABY
BOWWOW
CANADA
DRUMS
GIG
GUITAR
HIMSELF
ICEHOCKEY
JUSTIN
KEYBOARD
MYWORLD
NEVER
ONETIME
ONTARIO
PRAY
SCOOTER
SHOULDBEME
STICKS
USHER

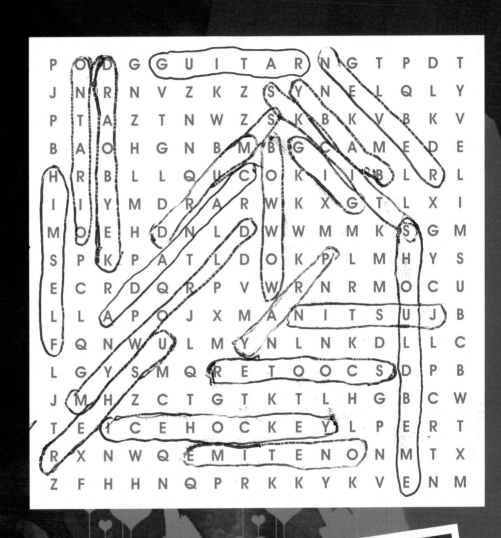

P O V D G G U I T A R N G T P D T
J N R N V Z K Z S Y N E L Q L Y
P T A Z T N W Z B K V B K V
B A O H G N M B C A M E D E
H R B L L Q U C O K I I B L R L
I I Y M D R A R W K X G T L X I
M O E H D N L D W M M K S G M
S P K P A T L D O K P L M H Y S
E C R D Q R P V W R N R M O C U
L L A P O J X M A N I T S U J B
F Q N W U L M Y N L N K D L L C
L G Y S M Q R E T O O C S D P B
J M H Z C T G T K T L H G B C W
T E I C E H O C K E Y L P E R T
R X N W Q E M I T E N O N M T X
Z F H H N Q P R K K Y K V E N M

JUSTIN'S
WORDSEARCH
23

we *love* you... Justin

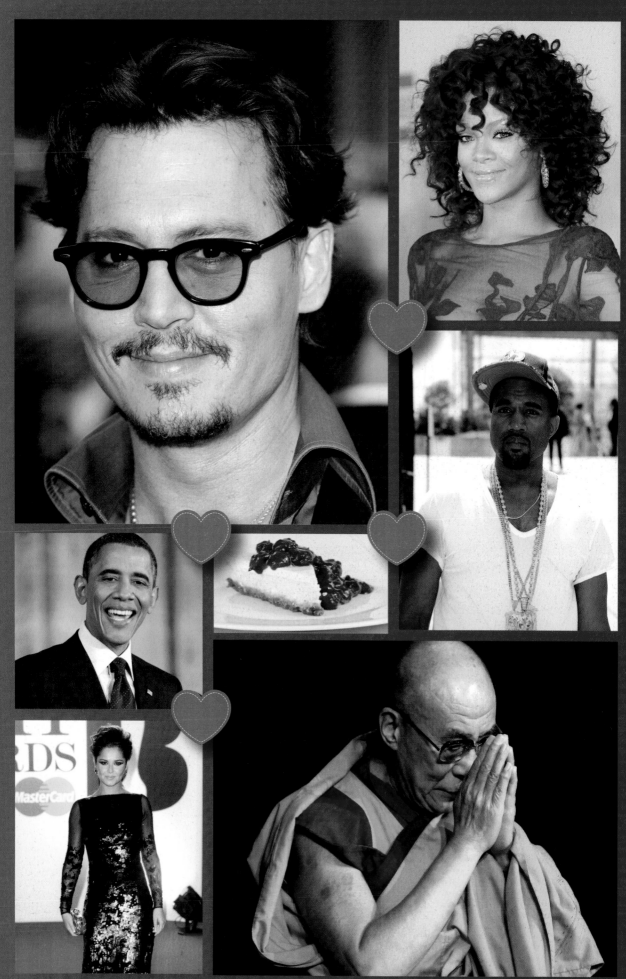

1   Before he became rich he slept on a blue pullout couch instead of a bed…

2   …and the house was full of mice!

3   One of his favourite foods is his Grandma's cherry cheesecake.

4   He boasted on Twitter about kissing Cheryl Cole and Rihanna backstage at the X Factor.

5   His Great Grandfather was a German immigrant to Canada.

6   Scooter Braun clicked on Justin's YouTube video by accident.

7   He crashed a Johnny Depp press conference to tell the Hollywood actor that he's a huge fan.

8   He revealed to the world that Kanye West doesn't use a mobile, just email.

9   He performed for President Obama at The White House at Christmas in 2009.

10 The UK Sunday newspaper reckons he is more influential in social networking (that means on Twitter and Facebook) than President Obama and the Dalai Lama!

10 THINGS YOU DIDN'T KNOW **ABOUT JUSTIN**

ICE, ICE HOCKEY!

You probably know that as a proud Canadian, Justin's favourite sport is ice hockey, or as he knows it, just 'hockey'.

As a super fan you probably also know that his favourite team is the Toronto Maple Leafs. But what else do you know about this sport that is almost a religion in Canada?

Here's a quick guide to put you in the picture:

The game is played on a rink between teams of six players, who try and score with a hard rubber puck. Each team has a well-protected goaltender (like a goalkeeper in football).

The first recognised, organised indoor match was played at the Victoria Skating Rink in Montreal in 1875.

The game is very big in Canada, USA, Russia and the Scandinavian countries.

The most well known competition is the Stanley Cup, played for by teams in the NHL (National Hockey League) which covers Canada and the USA.

The Montreal Canadiens with 34, have won the most Stanley Cups.

Justin's team the Toronto Maple Leafs have won the third most overall – 21 times.

A Canadian team has not won the Stanley Cup since the Canadiens in 1993.

The Boston Bruins are the current holders.

"Stay humble."

"I'm just a regular 16 year old kid. I make good grilled cheese and I like girls."

JUSTIN IN HIS OWN WORDS!

"I'm telling you, people. Every day we wake up is another blessing. Follow your dreams and don't let anyone stop you. Never say never."

"I want my world to be fun. No parents, no rules, no nothing. Like, no one can stop me. No one can stop me."

"I'm looking forward to influencing others in a positive way. My message is you can do anything if you just put your mind to it."

"If I can do just one tenth of the good Michael Jackson did for others, I can really make a difference in this world."

"My world got very big, very fast, and based on a lot of sad examples from the past, a lot of people expect me to get lost in it."

"A girl has to have a beautiful smile, beautiful eyes and she should have a good sense of humour. She should be honest, loving and trustworthy."

"I think older people can appreciate my music because I really show my heart when I sing, and it's not corny. I think I can grow as an artist, and my fans will grow with me."

we love you... Justin

THE ALBUM

Name:	My World 2.0
Released:	March 19, 2010
Length:	37:37
The Songs:	Baby
	Somebody to Love
	Stuck in the Moment
	U Smile
	Runaway Love
	Never Let You Go
	Overboard
	Eeenie Meenie
	UP
	That Should be Me
Achievements:	Debuted at Number one on US charts, selling over 283,000 copies.
	Justin was the youngest male solo act to top the US chart since Stevie Wonder in 1963.
	Justin then became the first performer since The Beatles to debut at number one and then sell more copies in the second week.
	My World 2.0 was number one in the USA, Ireland, Australia and New Zealand.

ALL THE ALBUMS!

ALL THE SINGLES!

THE SINGLES

Name	Released	UK Charts	USA Chart
One Time	May 18 2009	11	17
One Less Lonely Girl	Oct 6 2009	62	16
Baby (feat. Ludacris)	Jan 18 2010	3	5
		(and Number 1 in France!)	
Somebody to Love	April 20 2010	33	15
U Smile	Aug 9 2010	98	27
Never Say Never	Jan 25 2011	34	8

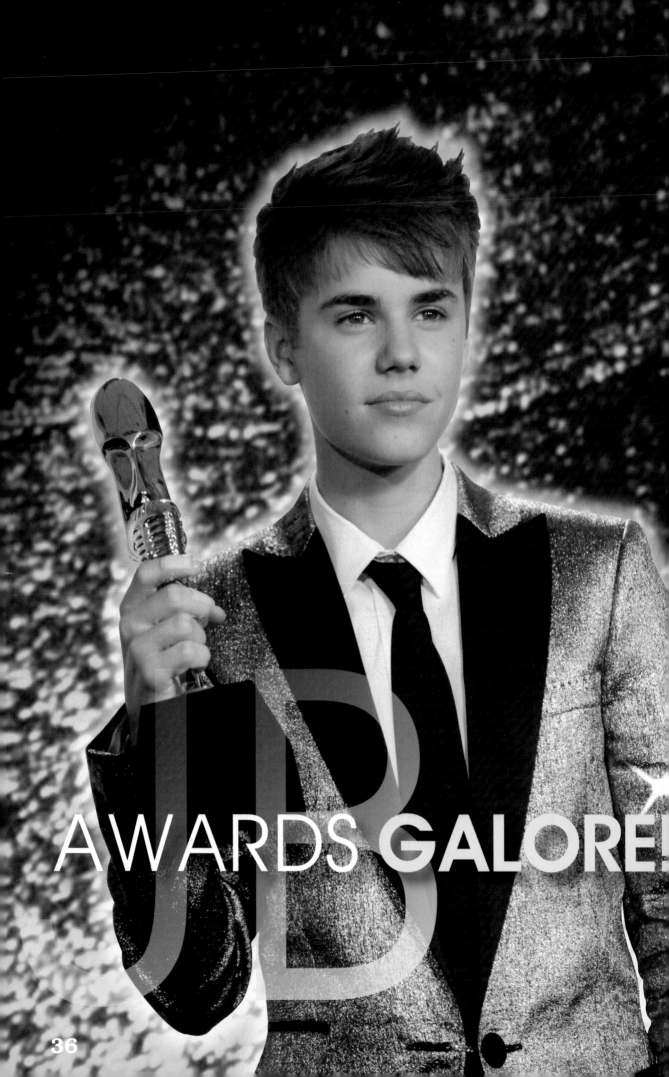

AWARDS GALORE!

In just two years on the international music scene Justin has collected more awards than many artists manage in a lifetime.

2012

4 American Music Awards including Artist of the Year

2 MTV Europe Music Awards including Best Male

MTV Video Music Award for Best New Artist

MTV Brazil Music Award for International Artist

4 Teen Choice Awards including Male Artist

Young Hollywood Award for Newcomer of the Year

2 World Music Award nominations

2011

6 Billboard Music Awards including Top Pop Album

2 Nickelodeon Kids' Choice Awards including Favourite Song

2 Juno Awards including Fan's Choice Award

Brit Award for International Breakthrough Act

2 Grammy nominations

and

NME Award for Worst Album! Cheek!

A is for: Atlanta, USA, where he first met Usher.

B is for: Baby, baby, baby please!

C is for: Canadian.

D is for: Drew, his middle name.

E is for: eBay, where he sold some of his hair for charity.

F is for: French Canadian ancestry, on his Mother's side.

G is for: Grammy Awards, which he presented in 2010.

H is for: Heartthrob!

I is for: Island, his record label

J is for: Jason, McCann, the character he played in CSI.

K is for: the Kiss he gave Selena Gomez at the 2011 Billboard Awards.

L is for: London, Ontario, Canada, his birthplace.

M is for: My World 2.0, the debut album.

N is for: Never Say Never.

O is for: One Time, the debut single.

P is for: Piano, one of the many instruments he taught himself.

Q is for: Quality, which his music is full of.

R is for: Raymond Braun Media, his first label.

S is for: Scooter. Raymond Braun's nickname.

T is for: Teen Idol.

U is for: Usher, his mentor.

V is for: Various music awards. 34 at the last count.

W is for: We are the World. In aid of Haitian earthquake victims.

X is for: X Factor UK. He performed live in 2010.

Y is for: YouTube, which made him a star.

Z is for: Zoology, an interest indulged by his support for the Gentle Barn Foundation.

A TO Z
OF JUSTIN!

Here's a list of all Justin's TV appearances, just in case you ever want to record them all…

ON THE SMALL SCREEN!

2009

As himself on:

True Jackson, VP
My Date With

2010

As a guest/performer on:

Saturday Night Live
X Factor UK
Hubworld

As himself on:

Silent Library
School Gyrls

As 'Jason McCann' on:

CSI: Crime Scene Investigation

2011

As a guest/performer on:

Saturday Night Live

As a guest/performer on:

Extreme Makeover;
Home Edition

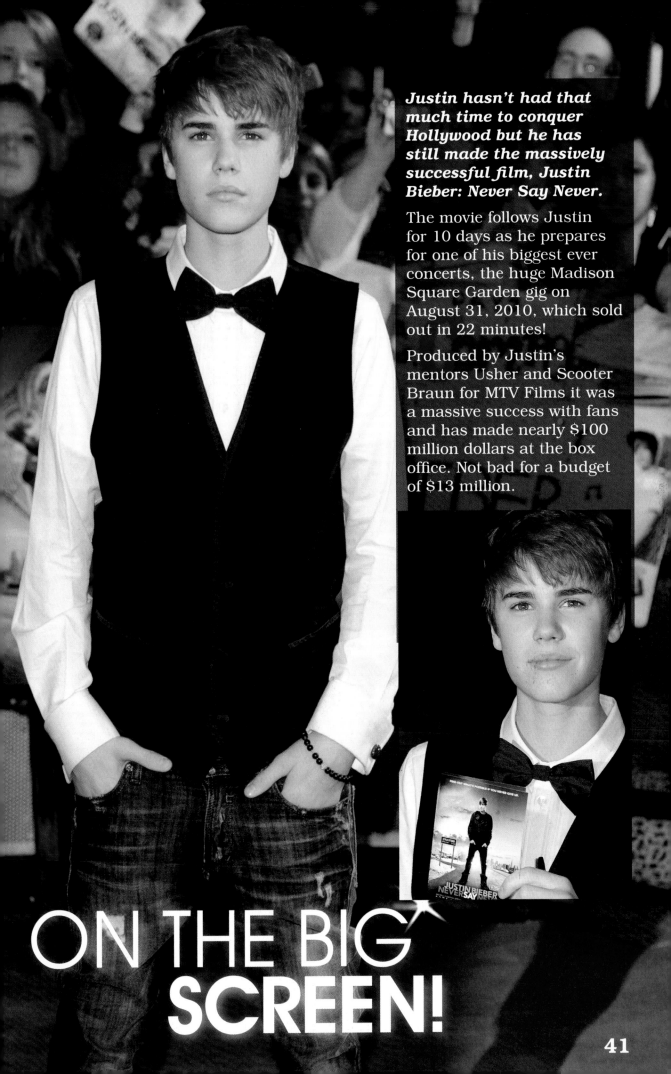

Justin hasn't had that much time to conquer Hollywood but he has still made the massively successful film, Justin Bieber: Never Say Never.

The movie follows Justin for 10 days as he prepares for one of his biggest ever concerts, the huge Madison Square Garden gig on August 31, 2010, which sold out in 22 minutes!

Produced by Justin's mentors Usher and Scooter Braun for MTV Films it was a massive success with fans and has made nearly $100 million dollars at the box office. Not bad for a budget of $13 million.

ON THE BIG SCREEN!

we *love* you... Justin

13	The age at which Justin flew to Atlanta to record his first demos.
25,024	The price in pounds, earned for charity by selling his hair on eBay.
98	The number of bidders in that auction.
90	The number of 'Personnel' associated with Justin as listed by Wikipedia.
53	Number of dollars, in millions, Justin earned 2010-11, according to Forbes magazine.

BIEBER BY NUMBERS!

6,000,000	Number of followers on Twitter according to their statistics in November 2010.
24,000	The number of followers per day he was reportedly gaining after November 2010.
283,000	The number of sales of My World 2.0 upon it's US release.
1.4	The number in millions of worldwide sales of My World 2.0.
2	The number of months those sales took.

NEVER SAY
NEVER...

10 THINGS JUSTIN WOULD NEVER DO....

There are some things that Justin would just never do. Here's a list of ten:

1. Go out without a comb...
2. ...and lots of emergency hair products!
3. Turn down the chance to learn a new instrument.
4. Fail to tweet to his fans at least a few times a week.
5. Stop working with other great artists like Chris Brown, Kanye West and Willow Smith.
6. Stop winning awards!
7. Be loved by the NME!
8. Stop making great music.
9. Stop dancing so well.
10. Stop performing huge, sell-out, entertaining shows.

NAME THAT TUNE...

Can you name these Justin Bieber songs with crucial words missing from the titles?

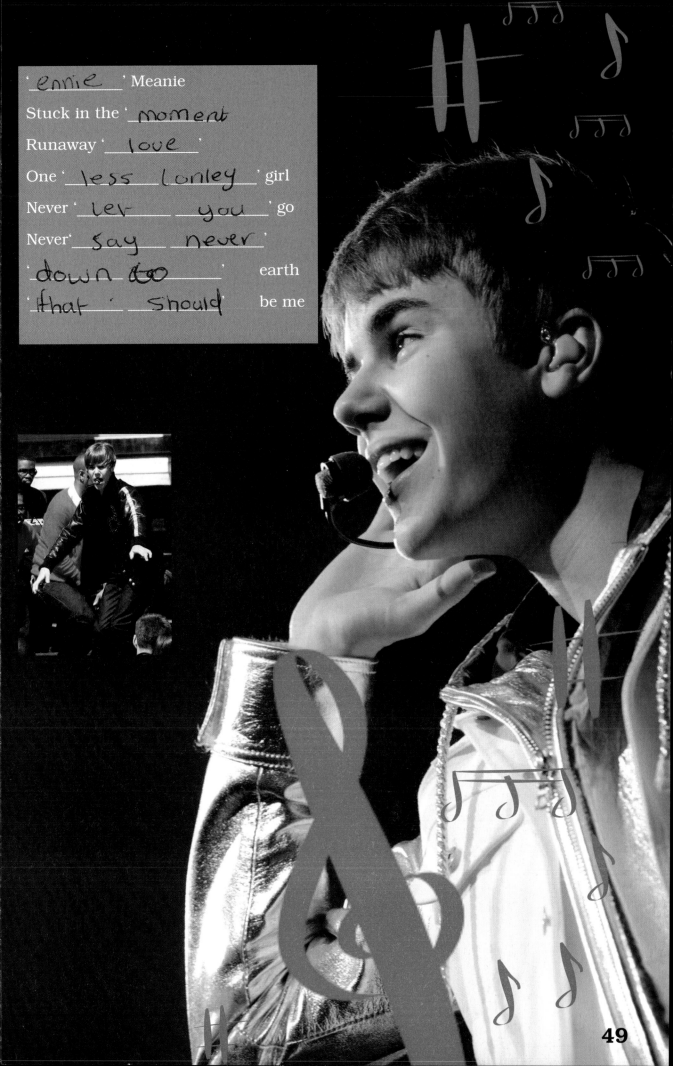

'_ennie_' Meanie
Stuck in the '_moment_'
Runaway '_love_'
One '_less lonley_' girl
Never '_let you_' go
Never '_say never_'
'_down to_' earth
'_that_' '_should_' be me

49

Whether it's wearing hoodies, sneakers, caps, urban or plaid shirts, Justin has so many great looks going on – here are just a few of your favourites...

50

STREETWISE
JUSTIN'S STYLE....

"Scooter" (real name "Scott") Braun is the man who was responsible for discovering Justin and is now his manager and mentor.

He came across one of the videos posted by Justin's mother Pattie on YouTube and arranged for him to fly to Atlanta to meet Usher.

Soon after, Scooter and Usher created the Raymond Braun Media Group and signed Justin up.

Scooter is 31 and was born in New York City. He went to Emory University in Atlanta and started his career by organising music events and parties for students, working with stars like Britney Spears and Ludacris.

In 2007 he started a record label called Schoolboy Records which launched the career of Asher Roth by releasing his first single *"I love college"* and his first album *"Asleep in the bread aisle"*.

Justin, Usher, MC Hammer and Jaden Smith all performed at his birthday party on June 18, 2011 at the Hollywood Music Box.

THE MEN BEHIND JUSTIN:
SCOOTER BRAUN

'Usher' (full name 'Usher Terry Raymond IV') was introduced to Justin by Scooter Braun in Atlanta and immediately saw how much talent he had. Usher has been Justin's musical mentor, manager and guide ever since.

He was born in Dallas but spent his childhood in Tennessee. He started to sing in church and began his musical career at the age of 11, (even younger than Justin!), in a group called NuBeginnings.

He is now one of the major recording artists in the world and his last three albums have all gone to number one in the US. Two of them: *Confessions* and *Here I Stand* were also UK number ones. He has also had eight number one singles in the US and four in the UK.

His occupations are listed on Wikipedia as: Singer-songwriter, music executive, actor, record producer, choreographer, dancer, composer, model, businessman, designer, and philanthropist!

THE MEN BEHIND JUSTIN:
USHER

Although during his youth Justin was a talented and popular athlete interested in ice hockey and soccer, he often kept his musical talent and aspirations to himself. He taught himself to play the piano, guitar and drums.

At the age of twelve, he sang Ne-Yo's So Sick at a local singing competition in his hometown of Stratford, Ontario. As every Bieber fan now knows, Justin came second but no-one remembers who won!

Pattie, Justin's mum, put a video of the performance on YouTube and began posting more videos after it became so popular. Scooter Braun, who had recently started his own record label, clicked on one of the videos by mistake. He was so impressed however, that he tracked down the theatre in Straford, Justin's school and finally his mum.

Not long after Justin flew to Atlanta, Georgia in the USA, to record some demo tapes with Scooter. He sang live for Usher and Antonio 'L.A.' Reid of Island Records and was promptly signed. Justin Timberlake had also shown a lot of interest.

So with Scooter as his manager and Usher as his musical mentor, teen idol Justin Bieber was ready to conquer the world!

HUMBLE BEGINNINGS
HOW IT ALL BEGAN

Though many young fans at first thought Justin was an American, he is of course a proud Canadian. "Canada is the best country in the world" he told Rolling Stone magazine. Here are 10 things he loves about his homeland:

1 As he also told Rolling Stone: Canada's free health service (just like the UK!).

2 His hometown of Stratford.

3 The Avon Theatre, where he first performed.

4 His home province of Ontario.

5 His favourite Ice Hockey team, the Toronto Maple Leafs.

6 Mike Myers, comedy actor and fellow Maple leafs fan.

7 His Mum!

8 His Grandma's cherry cheesecake

9 It's a place he can still relax in.

10 Maple syrup...(OK, that's just a guess!).

OH, CANADA!

15 SPOT THE DIFFERENCE
Did you spot them all?

17 QUIZ ANSWERS

1. Stratford, Ontario
2. Hartford, Connecticut
3. Drew
4. Birmingham
5. Will Smith
6. Pisces
7. Pattie
8. One Time
9. Ludacris
10. Haiti

11. The X Factor
12. Justin Bieber: Never Say Never
13. International Breakthrough Artist
14. 2
15. Teen Idol
16. That Should Be Me
17. Vancouver
18. Island Records
19. Someday
20. Liverpool

```
P O D G G U I T A R N G T P D T
J N R N V Z K Z S Y N E L Q L Y
P T A Z T N W Z S K B K V B K V
B A O H G N B M B G C A M E D E
H R B L L Q U C O K I I B L R L
I I Y M D R A R W K X G T L X I
M O E H D N L D W W M M K S G M
S P K P A T L D O K P L M H Y S
E C R D Q R P V W R N R M O C U
L L A P O J X M A N I T S U J B
F Q N W U L M Y N L N K D L L C
L G Y S M Q R E T O O C S D P B
J M H Z C T G T K T L H G B C W
T E I C E H O C K E Y L P E R T
R X N W Q E M I T E N O N M T X
Z F H H N Q P R K K Y K V E N M
```

49 NAME THAT TUNE

1. Eenie Meanie
2. Stuck in the Moment
3. Runaway Love
4. One Less Lonely Girl
5. Never Let You Go
6. Never Say Never
7. Down to Earth